The Crafter's Design Library

Fairies

Sharon Bennett

D&C
David and Charles

... and this is for Terry John... thank you

A DAVID & CHARLES BOOK
Copyright © David & Charles Limited 2008

David & Charles is an F+W Publications Inc. company
4700 East Galbraith Road
Cincinnati, OH 45236

First published in the UK in 2008
First US paperback edition 2008

Text and illustrations copyright © Sharon Bennett 2008

A catalogue record for this book is available from the British Library.

ISBN-13: 978-0-7153-2714-2 hardback
ISBN-10: 0-7153-2714-3 hardback

ISBN-13: 978-0-7153-2715-9 paperback
ISBN-10: 0-7153-2715-1 paperback

Printed in China by SNP Leefung for David & Charles
Brunel House, Newton Abbot, Devon

Commissioning Editor   Jane Trollope
Project Editor   Betsy Hosegood
Desk Editor   Demelza Hookway
Assistant Designer   Joanna Ley
Production Controller   Kelly Smith

Visit our website at www.davidandcharles.co.uk

David & Charles books are available from all good bookshops; alternatively you can contact our Orderline on 0870 9908222 or write to us at FREEPOST EX2 110, D&C Direct, Newton Abbot, TQ12 4ZZ (no stamp required UK only); US customers call 800-289-0963 and Canadian customers call 800-840-5220.

contents

the essential techniques

the templates

Fairy Fascination

There is something undeniably special about fairies. Creatures of the hidden realms, they are linked to woody dells, sunlight and shadows. They are friends to children and those in need, and have special powers to entice, punish or reward those they meet. They can be astoundingly delicate and beautiful and, of course, they can fly. No wonder we hold them in such fascination.

Fairies play a big part in our childhood, appearing as they do in books, films and verbal tales. We see them in plays too, as in *A Midsummer Night's Dream* and even ballets – *The Nutcracker*. These were not written just with children in mind, for the truth is that adults love fairy stories too.

This was brought home in 1917 when two cousins, Elsie Wright and Frances Griffiths produced the most famous photographs of fairies ever taken in Britain. Elsie and Frances claimed they had seen fairies but of course no one believed

them, so Elsie borrowed her father's plate camera, got some basic instructions and disappeared down to the beck behind the house in Cottingley with her cousin where they took some pictures to 'prove' their story. Eventually the pictures were published but were they real? Many people thought so, including Sir Arthur Conan Doyle who created Sherlock Holmes, and the photographs were studied by experts while the world waited hopefully. The fact is that we *want* to believe in fairies.

So what are fairies like? Well the answer is that there are many kinds of fairies and fairy folk, hence the wide range of motifs in this book. To start with, let's begin with the cute imps and delightful young fairies inspired by illustrations from childhood tales, including Arthur Rackham's colour plates for the first edition of *Peter Pan* (see page 28).

Famous among the fairies are Tinkerbell and her friends, the fairy godmothers in *Cinderella* and *Sleeping Beauty*, the tooth fairy and the Cottingley fairies as pictured by Frances and Elsie (see pages 48–59). Next we look at seasonal fairies (page 60), who dance and leap on moonbeams, shelter under spring bluebells or daisies or can be found on toadstools or in the briar bushes in the autumn. Of course, the most famous seasonal fairy of all sits on top of the Christmas tree.

Then we have the fairies and other supernatural figures from stories – there's Thumbelina and the Little Mermaid, Snow White, Cinderella and her fairy godmother.

There's even a section on fairy land (see page 98) with ideas for potential dwellings, fairy transport, eating, dancing, washing and dating. The finishing touches section (page 114), which completes this book, contains useful borders, banners, an alphabet and more.

If you get stuck for ideas for using the fairy motifs, see pages 6–13 to help you get started and pages 14–25 for some delightful fairy projects. All in all, there's plenty of fun to be had creating and discovering fairies in this book.

Applying motifs to craft media

The techniques best suited to applying your selected motif to a particular medium depend on the surface you are working with. The following pages offer some simple advice on how to do this for the most popular craft media. Guidance is also given on how to enlarge or reduce the motif to suit your requirements (below) and how to create a stencil (page 11).

Enlarging and reducing a motif

Here are three ways to change the size of a motif to suit your project: the traditional method using a grid, or the modern alternatives of a photocopier or scanner.

Using a grid

The traditional method of enlargement involves using a grid. To begin, use low-tack masking tape to secure tracing paper over the original design. Draw a square or rectangle onto the tracing paper, enclosing the image (see below). Use a ruler to divide up the square or rectangle into rows of equally spaced vertical and horizontal lines. Complex designs should have lines about 1cm (³⁄₈in) apart; simpler ones can have lines 4cm (1½in) apart.

Now draw a square or rectangle to match your required design size, and draw a grid to correspond with the one you have just drawn over the image, as shown below. You can now begin to re-create the original image by redrawing it, square by square, at the required scale.

Using a photocopier

For fast and accurate results, use a photocopier to enlarge or reduce a motif. To do this, you need to calculate your enlargement percentage. First measure the width of the image you want to end up with. Here, the motif needs to be enlarged to 120mm (4¾in). Measure the width of the original motif, which in this case is 80mm (3¼in). Divide the first measurement by the second to find the percentage by which you need to enlarge the motif, in this instance 150%. (An enlargement must always be more than 100% and a reduction less than 100%).

To photocopy an image onto tracing paper, use tracing paper that is at least 90gsm. When photocopying an image from tracing paper, place the tracing paper onto the glass, and then lay a sheet of white paper on top of it. This will help to produce a sharp copy.

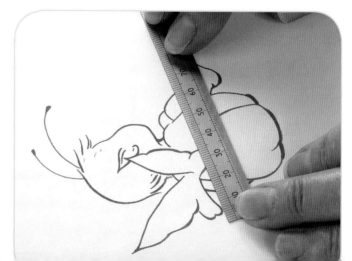

Transferring a motif onto paper, card, wood or fine fabric

A light box makes it easy to trace an image directly onto a piece of paper, thin card or fabric, but if you don't have one it is easy to improvize with household items. Balance a piece of clear plastic across two piles of books or pieces of furniture, and place a table lamp underneath. Place your motif on the plastic and your paper, thin card or fabric on top. Switch on the light and simply trace over the design showing through.

To transfer a design onto wood, thick card or foam, trace the design onto tracing paper using a sharp pencil. Turn the tracing over and redraw on the wrong side with a soft lead pencil. Now turn the tracing over again and use masking tape to secure it right side up onto your chosen surface. Carefully redraw the image (see the photograph below). Press firmly enough to transfer the motif, but take care not to damage the surface.

Using a scanner

A third way to enlarge or reduce a motif is to scan the original image on a flatbed scanner or to photograph it with a digital camera. Once the image is on your computer you can either adjust the size using image manipulation software or simply alter the percentage of your printout size. If the finished result is larger than the printer's capacity, some software will allow you to tile the image over several sheets of paper, which can then be joined together to form the whole image.

An image-manipulation package may also allow you to alter the proportions of a motif, making it wider or narrower, for example. Take care not to distort it beyond recognition, though. Once you are happy with your image, it can be saved to be used again and again.

Transferring a motif onto foil

To emboss foil, simply take the original tracing and secure it to the foil surface. Rest the foil on kitchen paper. Use an embossing tool or an old ballpoint pen that has run out of ink to press down on the tracing, embossing the metal below. Use the same technique on the back of the foil to produce a raised effect.

Transferring a motif onto mirror and ceramic

Trace the motif onto tracing paper, then turn the tracing over and redraw it on the wrong side using a chinagraph pencil. A chinagraph produces a waxy line that adheres well to shiny surfaces such as coloured glass, mirrored glass and ceramic. Chinagraphs are prone to blunt quickly, but it doesn't matter if the lines are thick and heavy at this stage. Use masking tape to secure the tracing right side up onto the surface. Carefully redraw with a sharp pencil to transfer the image.

Tracing a motif onto glass and acetate

Roughly cut out the motif and tape it to the underside of the acetate or glass with masking tape. It is helpful to rest glassware on a few sheets of kitchen towel for protection and to stop curved objects from rolling. The image will now show through the clear surface, and you can simply trace along the lines with glass outliner or paint directly onto the surface.

If you want to transfer an image onto opaque glass, or onto a container that is difficult to slip a motif behind, such as a bottle with a narrow neck, follow the instructions on page 7 for transferring a motif onto mirror and ceramic.

Transferring a motif onto curved items

Motifs can be transferred onto rounded items, but will need to be adapted to fit the curves. First trace the motif, redrawing it on the underside (use a chinagraph pencil if the container is ceramic). Make cuts in the template from the edge towards the centre. Lay the motif against the surface so that the cuts slightly overlap or spread open, depending on which way the surface curves. Tape the motif in place with masking tape and transfer the design by drawing over the lines with a sharp pencil.

Making a template for a straight-sided container

If you wish to apply a continuous motif such as a border to a straight-sided container, make a template of the container first. To do this, slip a piece of tracing paper into a transparent glass container or around an opaque glass or ceramic container. Lay the paper smoothly against the surface and tape in place with masking tape. Mark the position of the upper edge of the container with a pencil. Now mark the position of the overlapping ends of the paper or mark each side of the handle on a mug, cup or jug.

Remove the tracing and join the overlap marks, if you have made these. Measure down from the upper edge and mark the upper limit of the band or border on the template. Cut out the template and slip it into or around the container again to check the fit. Transfer your chosen template onto the tracing paper, then onto the container.

Making a template for a plate

1 Cut a square of tracing paper slightly larger than the diameter of the plate. Make a straight cut from one edge to the centre of the paper then roughly cut out a circle from the centre to help the paper lie flat. Place the paper centrally on the plate or saucer and tape one cut edge across the rim. Smooth the paper around the rim and tape in place, overlapping the cut edges. Mark the position of the overlap on the paper.

2 Turn the plate over and draw around the circumference onto the underside of the tracing paper. Remove the paper, then measure the depth of the plate rim and mark it on the paper by measuring in from the circumference. Join the marks with a curved line.

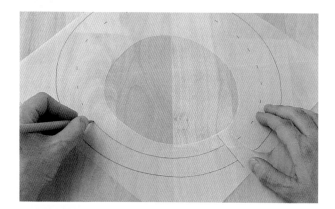

Transferring a motif onto fabric

If fabric is lightweight and pale in colour, it may be possible to trace the motif simply by laying the fabric on top. If the fabric is dark or thick, it may help to use a light box. Place the motif under the fabric on the surface of the light box (see page 7 for information on constructing a home light box). As the light shines up through the motif and fabric you should be able to see the design lines, ready for tracing.

Alternatively, place a piece of dressmaker's carbon paper face down on the fabric and tape the motif on top with masking tape. Trace the design with a sharp pencil to transfer it onto the fabric, as shown below. The marks made by the carbon are easily wiped away.

Transferring a motif onto a knitting chart

Use knitting-chart paper rather than ordinary graph paper to chart a knitting design. (Knitted stitches are wider than they are tall and knitting chart paper is sized accordingly.) Transfer the motif straight onto the knitting graph paper (see page 7 for advice on transferring onto paper). Each square on the graph paper represents a stitch. Make sure that you are happy with the number of squares in the motif, as this dictates the number of stitches in your design, and ultimately the design size. Fill in the applicable squares on the chart using coloured pens or pencils. (Note: this fairy is going on a scarf that is knitted sideways, so the fairy is plotted sideways too.)

Use the finished chart in conjunction with a knitting pattern. Read the chart from right to left for a knit row and from left to right for a purl row. The motif can also be worked with Swiss darning.

Transferring a motif onto needlepoint canvas and cross stitch fabric

Designs on needlepoint canvas and cross-stitch fabric can be worked either by referring to the design on a chart, or by transferring the image to the material and stitching over it.

To transfer the motif onto a chart

Transfer the motif straight onto graph paper (see page 7 for advice on transferring onto paper). Each square on the graph paper represents a square of canvas mesh or Aida cross-stitch fabric. Colour in the squares that the motif lines cross with coloured pencils or pens. You may want to make half stitches where the motif outline runs through a box. Mark the centre of the design along a vertical and horizontal line (see right) and mark the centre of the fabric lengthways and widthways with tacking stitches.

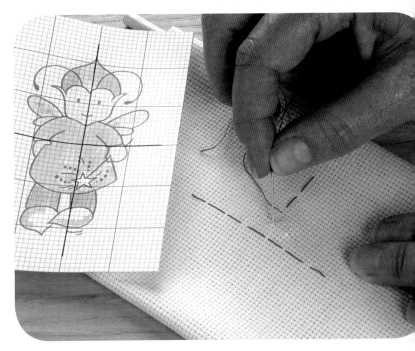

To transfer the motif directly onto canvas or fabric

With an open-weave canvas or pale fabric it is possible to trace the design directly onto the canvas or fabric. First, mark a small cross centrally on the motif and on the material. On a light box (see page 7), place the material on top of the motif, aligning the crosses. Tape in position and trace the image with a waterproof pen. Alternatively, use dressmaker's carbon paper to transfer the design, as explained in transferring a motif onto fabric, opposite.

Making a stencil

Tape a piece of tracing paper over the motif to be adapted into a stencil. Redraw the image, thickening the lines and creating 'bridges' between the sections to be cut out. You may find it helpful to shade in the areas to be cut out. Lay a piece of carbon paper, ink side down, on a stencil sheet, place the tracing on top, right side up, and tape in place. Redraw the design to transfer it to the stencil sheet. Finally, lay the stencil sheet on a cutting mat and carefully cut out the stencil with a craft knife, always drawing the sharp edge of the blade away from you.

Adapting and combining designs

Although you can use the templates in this book exactly as they are, a lot of fun is to be had simply messing around with them, simplifying designs, making them more ornate, combining them and so on. You can do this endlessly, making your library of templates never-ending as your ideas become new images.

A quick way of changing a motif is either to simplify it or to add greater detail. Try enlarging or reducing the dots on a toadstool, making a fairy's hair longer or changing the direction of her eyes, for example. Another idea is to embellish a fairy's garments, as shown right, where the clothing of the original fairy motif from page 52 (far right) has been embellished with dots, swirls and curls.

Mix and match

Take sections from different fairy motifs to create a new one. As long as you make them the same scale, this is often quite easy. The flying fairy, near right, has the wings and upper body of the fairy with the heart on page 65 but the skirt and legs of the fairy at the top right of page 55. Meanwhile the seated fairy, far right, can be found on page 95, but her wings are from a fairy on page 109. See how many new fairies you can create in this way – it's great fun.

Shapes and border

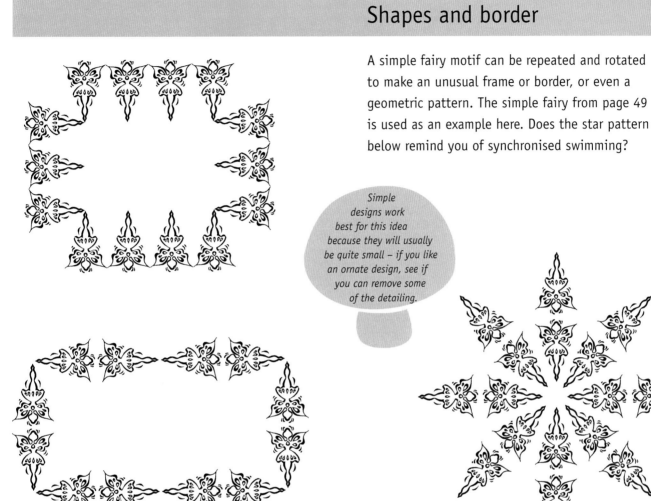

A simple fairy motif can be repeated and rotated to make an unusual frame or border, or even a geometric pattern. The simple fairy from page 49 is used as an example here. Does the star pattern below remind you of synchronised swimming?

Simple designs work best for this idea because they will usually be quite small – if you like an ornate design, see if you can remove some of the detailing.

Flip it

Motifs can work well if you use the original plus a mirror image, created by flipping the design. Here, the fairy at the bottom of page 110 and a silhouetted version of the same fairy show how it's done. This idea works well if you put a fairy in each corner of a card, for example, or one on each side of a banner or central motif, such as one of the dwellings on pages 102–103.

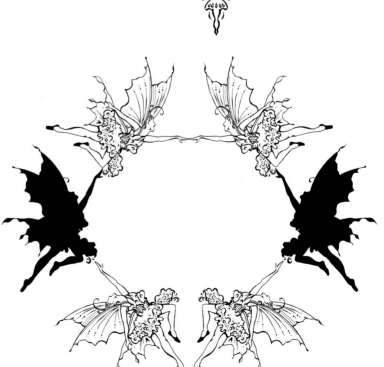

Techniques and mediums

Trying out different techniques and mediums is a good way of stretching your creativity, so don't limit yourself to the same materials you've always used – take the opportunity to try something new. Here's just a sample to whet your appetite.

Embossing

These days many of us use a stencil for embossing, but this isn't strictly necessary. Trace your fairy image, turn over the tracing and lay it on foil or vellum. Place both layers on a piece of stiff foam, such as an upturned mouse mat, and go over the lines carefully, without pressing too hard. Now just turn over the foil or vellum and apply it to your card or other item. Here, the sleeping fairy from page 45 was embossed onto rainbow vellum and then glued to a plain white card.

When working with vellum, it is better to go over the design lines twice quite lightly than to press hard and risk tearing the paper.

Stencilling

This is an easy and enjoyable way of using a motif. Make your stencil as explained on page 11, making sure you keep the cut-away sections separate so that a big piece of your design doesn't just drop out. Use a stencil brush or sponge to dab small amounts of acrylic paint onto the surface to be stencilled, using more than one colour, if desired. Add further embellishments as desired.

Combining papers

Making a motif from several different papers can be lots of fun. Simply trace and cut out each section of your fairy from a different paper, as shown here. Now assemble the layers, starting with those at the back and building up to the details; stick the layers in place. Now you can add detailing with outliners, stick-on gems and so on. This fairy motif can be found on page 34.

Avoid unsightly gaps between sections by extending some pieces where they are hidden behind others. For example the wings could meet behind the fairy and the arms could be joined behind the dress.

Fabric painting

There are many fabric paints available on the market but most are designed for either silk or cotton. Silk should be stretched in a frame first, and the design lines drawn with gutta. Once this is dry you can flood silk paint into areas enclosed by a gutta line. Acrylic fabric paints can be used like paint on fabric – sponged, applied with a brush or drawn on. The fairy on the right (see page 31) was painted onto blue voile using silver glitter paint and stretched and glued to white card. A limited use of blue paint adds tonal variation.

Gutta is great for adding texture – don't just use it to create areas for painting, use it for the details too.

Using a computer

For quick collage, scan images into a computer and print out repeated motifs to cut out and stick down. You can change the colour on the computer or use pens and paints to embellish them later. If desired, you can stick the motifs down with sticky pads to raise them off the surface. The motifs used here can be found on pages 55 and 32.

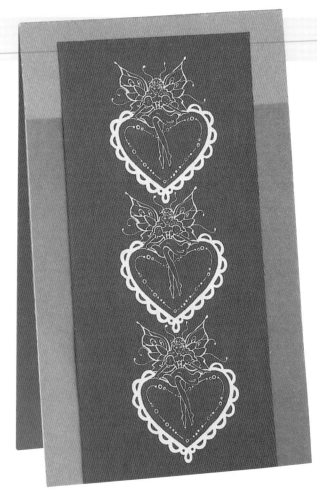

Reversing out

This technique is easiest to do on a computer by making the motif white and laying it over an area of colour. Alternatively, you can trace the motif onto coloured paper or card and then paint over the lines with white pen, paint or outliner. Another idea is to trace your design onto white paper, cut it out and stick it onto a coloured base, rather like a white silhouette. The motif used here is on the top right of page 65.

Tonal images

This pixie (see page 30) has been painted in watercolour in shades of green. Using just one colour in different tones can look stylish and sophisticated, especially when combined with card or embellishments in the same colour. In watercolour you can just dilute the paint to make lighter and lighter colours, but with other mediums you could add white paint. Adding white gives a creamy effect to the colours and provides flat coverage whereas diluting with water creates translucency.

With this technique, each section – wings, clothing, face – doesn't have to be a flat tone. You can create more interest with variety as in the examples here.

Using outliners

Outliners aren't just for silk fabrics and ceramics – they work fabulously well on paper too. This fairy, from page 34, was traced and coloured with marker pen, and then the detailing was added with pretty silver outliner. Make sure you leave the outliner to dry for sufficient time before handling the design – you don't want to smudge it at this stage.

Transfer the main design lines to paper so you can colour them in, but leave out the detailing. Colour the design then place the paper on a light box over the original template. Now you can simply trace on the details with the outliner.

Choosing a medium

Deciding which surface you are going to paint on is the first step in any project. Then you have to look at what paints are suitable and consider the effect you want to achieve. Crafting really does take over so make sure you set aside a clear space to work in and have plenty of time.

Metallic and pearlized paints

Metallic and pearlized paints lend themselves really well to this subject of fairies, especially when it comes to their wings, which look super when they are reflective. The example here uses a motif from page 67 that has been painted with interference paints. These are iridescent and work when the light catches them to shimmer and glint. Look out for glitter sealers too, which are clear based and dry to a matt finish but have tiny glitter particles in them that sing out in silver, gold or pearl.

Metal leaf

Usually metal leaf is applied by first painting glue size onto the area to be treated and then applying the metal leaf on top. Another way is to apply the glue as an outliner and then press on special foil, and this was what was done to create the fairy shown here. Sometimes you need to apply a hairdryer to complete the process, so check with the manufacturer's instruction. Here, the foiled fairy was attached to a complementary card using sticky foam pads. See page 52 for this fairy.

If you are planning to cut out your motif, as here, you may find it easier to do this before you add the foil detailing – that way you can get the foil right up to the edges.

Crayons and pencils

Here the cute daisy imp (page 67) has been traced onto textured paper that is suitable for use with coloured pencils and then coloured in. A good trick here is to colour in the design, scan it into a computer and then print it out at reduced size. That way everyone will think you have managed to create amazing detail! Add further detailing and texture to your work with outliner, or look out for water-soluble pencils, which can be washed over with a wet paintbrush to spread the colour.

Pen and ink

The Sugar Plum Fairy from page 49 has been used for a very graphic result on the card here. Outline the design in waterproof pen first and then colour in with inks. Notice how well the bright colours of the inks work with a strong design like this. The same process was used for the tag.

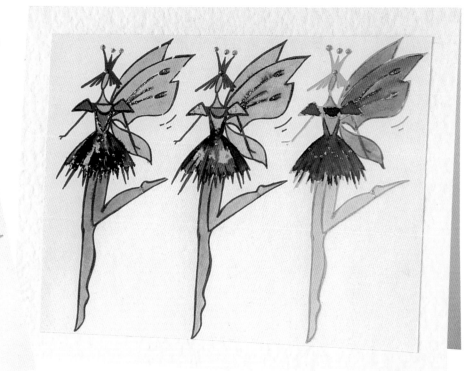

Project gallery

Card making is probably the number one use for the templates in this book, but there are times when you will want to treat a friend, yourself or your home to something creative and special. Here are some ideas for using the templates for a variety of items.

Nearly any card would also make a great tag, so to coordinate you gift, make a tag to match – or see the tip below.

blue fairy

Pop-up cards are always well received. To make this greetings card, transfer the fairy from page 55 onto a rectangle of white card so that her chin is about halfway up. Decorated the bottom half of the card and the fairy with paints and stick-ons. Now score the card in half, stopping at each side of the fairy. Using a craft knife on a cutting mat, cut out the fairy above the fold line. Fold the card and the fairy should stand up.

yellow fairy

This wonderful card shows some clever uses of outliner. First the fairy was traced onto watercolour paper and coloured in with watercolour paints. Then she was outlined with black outliner and the right of the card was trimmed away. The yellow area was also painted with watercolour paints and then embellished with dots of pearly outliner, adding a super three-dimensional quality.

Don't forget that you can scan a coloured image into a computer and then print it out again and again at any size, perhaps to make a tag or giftwrap.

flowerpot fairies

These cards show how different a design can look depending on how you use it. The card on the far left is covered with rainbow vellum, applied with spray glue and then embellished with flowers and a little glitter glue. The card shown near left was made in two parts with crackled brown card for the pot and painted white card for the fairy. Again, glitter glue adds fairy sparkle.

Cinderella's slipper

For this clever card, the shoe from page 89 was enlarged, traced onto pink metallic card and then stuck onto plain white card. The plain card was embellished with pale pink swirls. The fairies from pages 88 and 65 were scanned into a computer, printed in pink and then coloured with pens before being attached to the slipper with craft foam pads. Notice how part of the heel of the slipper has been cut away for added interest.

card-saver wallet

Simple motifs, like the fairy from page 64, make great all-over designs. For this card-saver the fairy was traced repeatedly onto paper and the background coloured in loosely. Add colour to some of the fairies for added variety. As you can see, this motif works well on tags, cards, folders and anything else you like.

stones

The fairy above (see page 66) was painted onto a pebble using acrylic paint, while the fairy on the right (see page 49) was created with white acrylic and mauve outliner.

You are no longer allowed to take stones from beaches, so look out for suitable substitutes in your garden or local park.

magic chest

Wooden boxes usually need to be primed before you paint over them. This small wooden chest was primed and then painted with rainbow colours. The silhouette motif from page 96 was added in black paint – the fairy on the lid is a cut-out that was added at the end (see page 105). A glittery sealer adds the finishing touch.

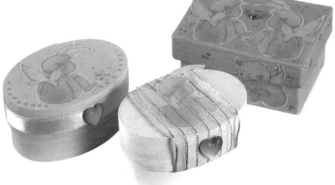

for the tooth fairy

Use the same idea as described above to decorate small card boxes, perhaps to encourage the tooth fairy to visit. This cherub fairy is on page 30.

fairy mug

It's great fun painting a design on a mug, and afterwards you'll be able to admire your handiwork every day. This fairy godmother, from page 52, was transferred to the mug as explained on page 7 and coloured with ceramic paints. Try to build up flat areas of colour and keep the paint application light.

fairy light

A lantern always adds atmosphere to an evening barbecue or alfresco dinner, and this one might even entice the fairies out to join you. This fairy, from page 38, has been applied to the windows with interference medium, which captures the magical quality of her wings. If this is to be a present, make a tag and card to match.

lotions and potions

Glass jars and vials can be painted with glass paints in exactly the same way as the lantern – though if they are small you will need a correspondingly tiny brush for the paintwork. The fairies used here are from pages 37 and 38.

Small beads can be dropped into some glass paints before they dry. The paint acts as a glue to hold the beads in place.

If you aren't very good at sewing, use outliner to pipe the design and stick beads on top.

fabric pouches

Fairies are great motifs for jewellery bags. You can paint them on, as on the pink bag, try some embroidery, or stitch the outlines with beads and sequins. Look out for glittery fabric paints and sparkling or pearly beads to enhance the fairy theme. The motifs used here come from pages 37 (painted pouch) and 53 (beaded pouches).

If you don't have any beads, just dab dots of outliner in pearlescent or metallic colours along the design lines.

card fairy

The idea suggested above can be used for a host of other items too. What about a fairy cushion for a little girl, for example? You could also make a card with beads as shown here, or even using stick-on gemstones. The motif used here can be found on page 53.

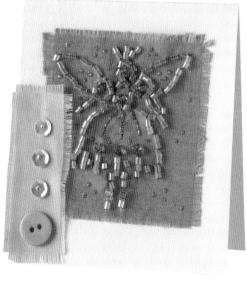

the
templates

Fairy Fun

Fairies and fairy folk often have a cheeky, impish side to them, and this chapter is all about them. These are the fun-loving, naughty and even trendy fairies that will appeal especially to the very young, to children and to teenagers.

The selection starts with some wonderful chubby-faced baby fairies, ideal for those baby-arrival and congratulations cards, or to celebrate a birthday or first tooth (see the boxes on page 23). Take a look at the birthday fairies on pages 34–37 too, with balloons, gifts and cakes for birthday girls of all ages.

Older girls, especially young teenagers, will love the stylish fairies towards the end of the chapter, while boys will enjoy the naughty elves and goblins on pages 32–33, which are sure to appeal to their impish side. And for a sick child, don't miss the bedtime fairies and story-telling imp on pages 44–45.

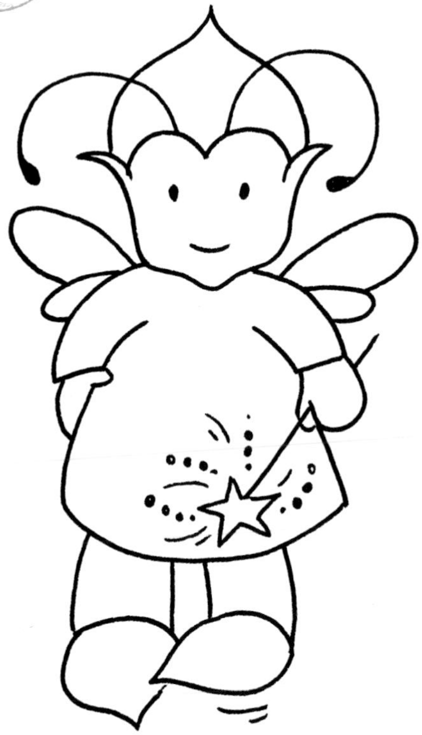

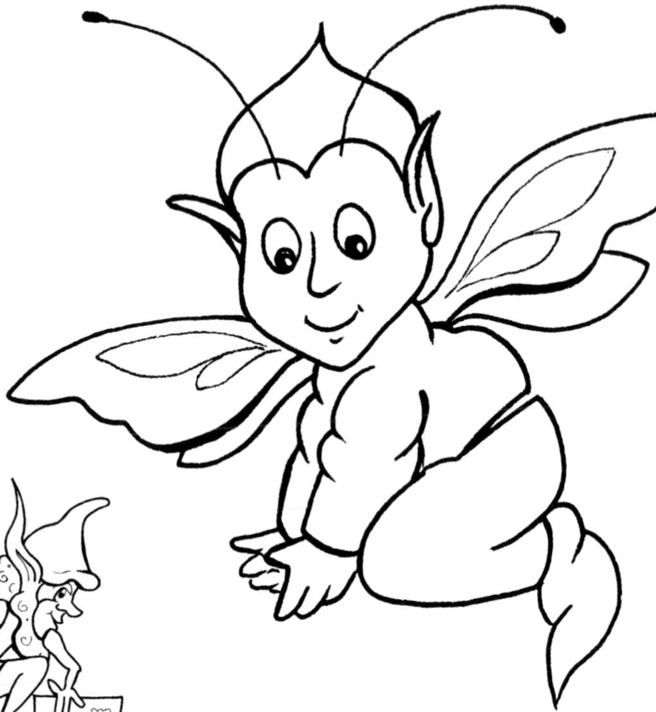

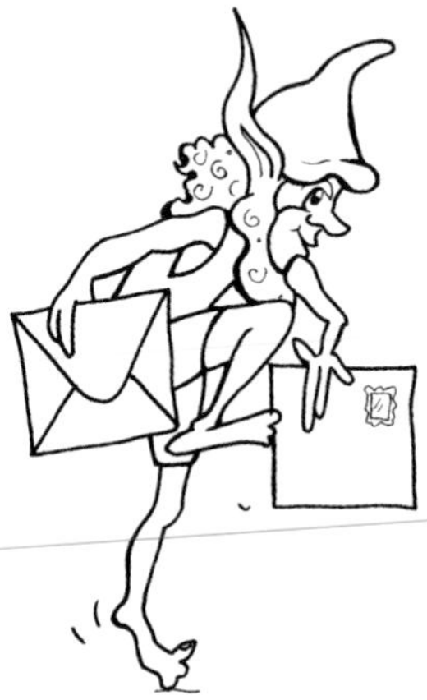

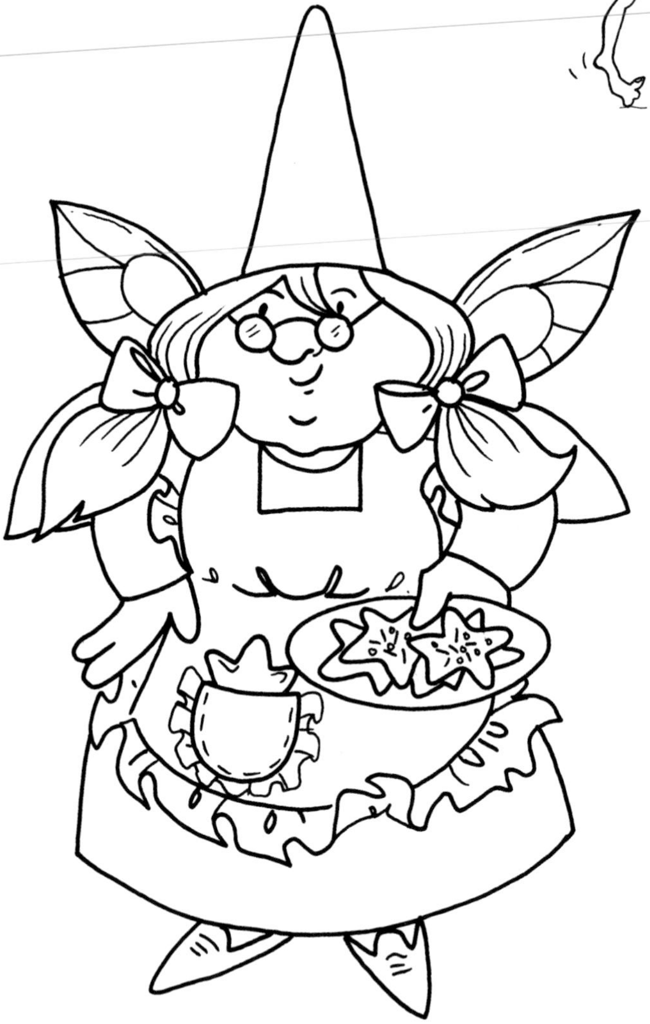

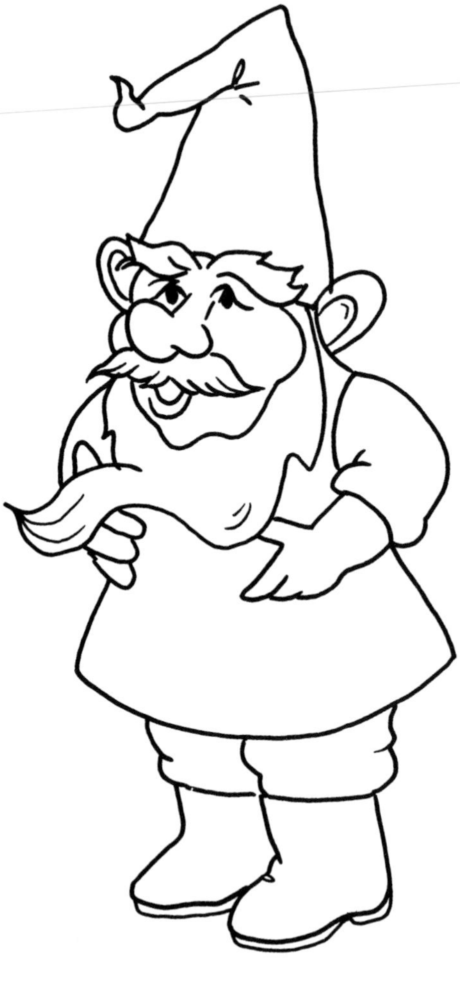

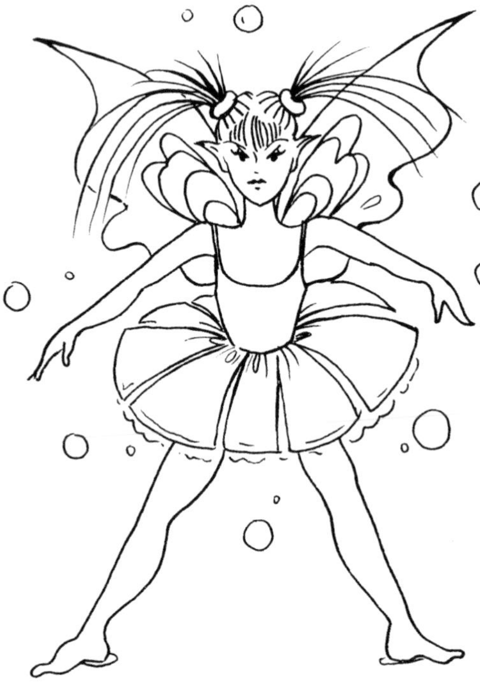

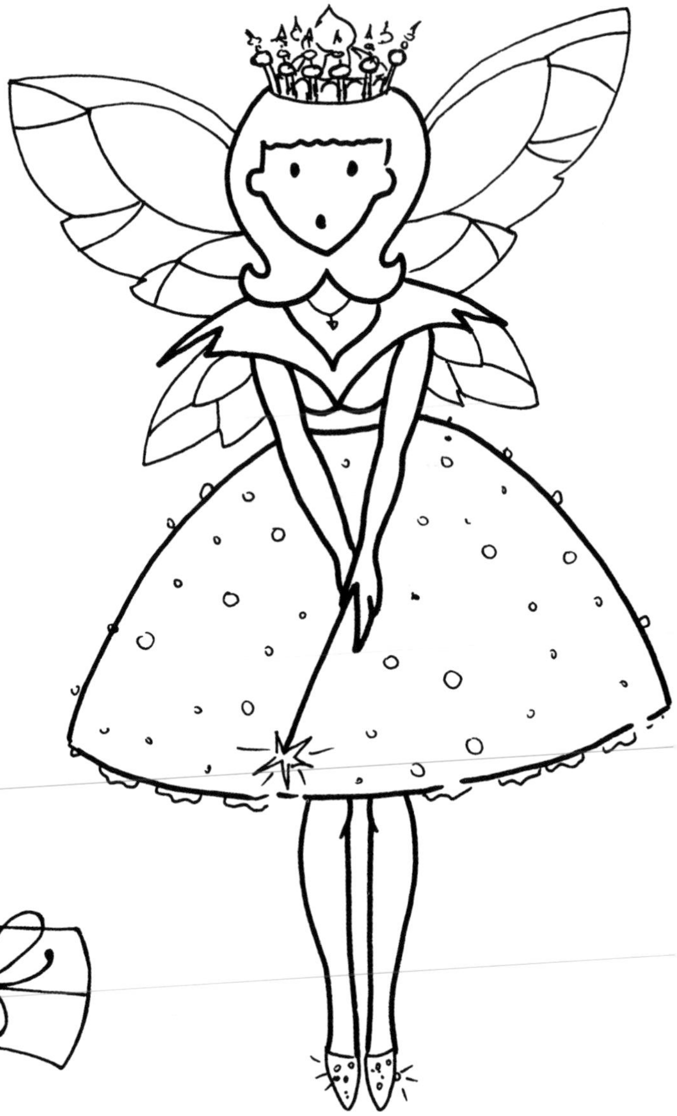

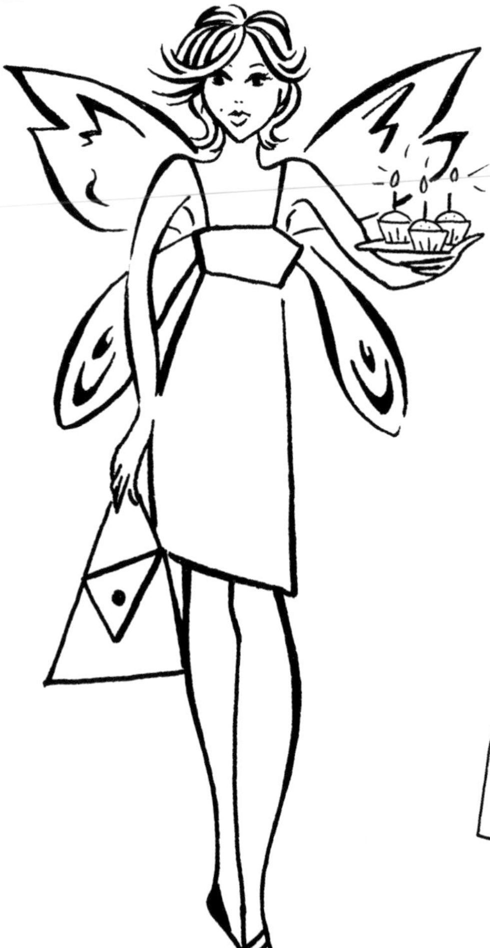

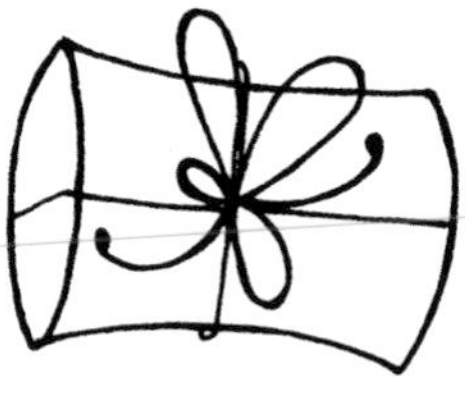

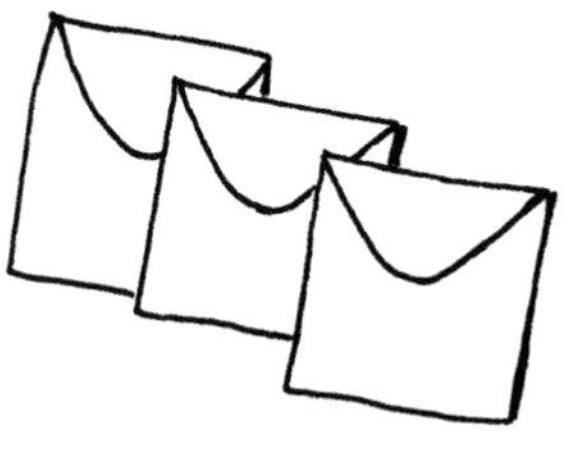

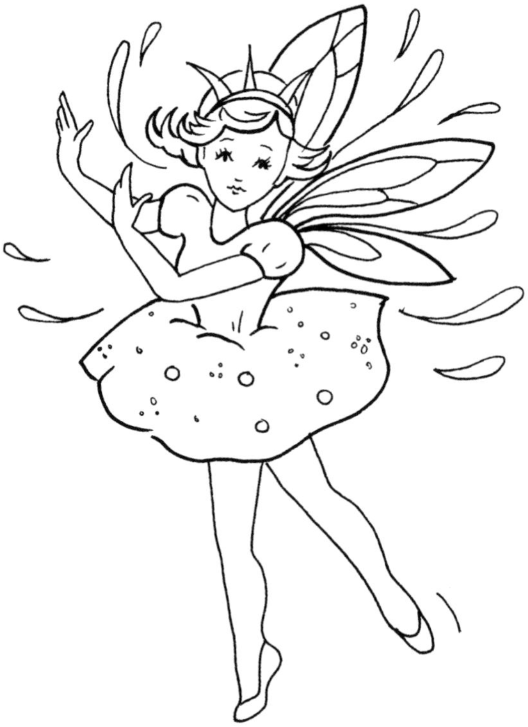

Famous Fairies

Role out the red carpet for the glitterati of fairy land. Here come Tinkerbell and the Sugar Plum Fairy, Cinderella's fairy godmother (pages 52–53), the tooth fairy (pages 54–55) and other glamorous characters we've heard of but perhaps find it difficult to visualize and put on to paper.

In 1917 the Cottingley fairies were made famous by two teenagers, Elsie Wright and Frances Griffiths, who showed photographs of themselves in the garden with some astoundingly beautiful fairies. Sceptics tested the picture negatives and found that they hadn't been faked, but no one thought to ask if the fairies were actually made of paper... These famous fairies are featured on pages 58–59.

And what should you do with these famous characters? Why send them to a budding star, of course, or to anyone in need of the services of a fairy godmother or a tooth fairy.

Seasonal Fairies

Fairies celebrate the changing of the seasons in so many ways, especially those that care for flowers and trees. Find the perfect sprite from the ones in this chapter to bring a little magic to the season, whether it be pretty spring floral fairies, or Jack Frost and his friends. And who else would you find at the top of the Christmas tree but a beautiful winged fairy?

No one knows more about matters of the heart than the romantic fairies featured on our Valentine's pages. They are perfect for decorating wedding gifts or making cards for anniversaries. The crafting calendar offers endless opportunities to create seasonal greetings and gifts for friends and family, and even the weather has a collection of fairy champions to help you brighten even the dullest rainy day.

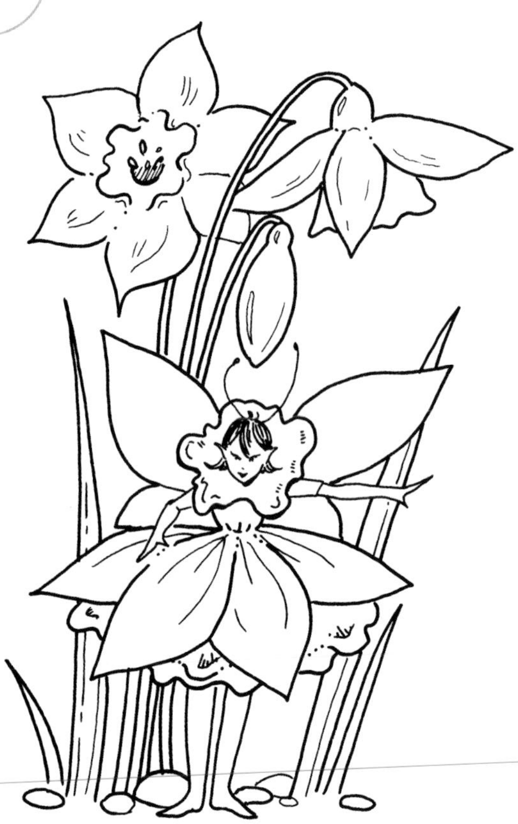
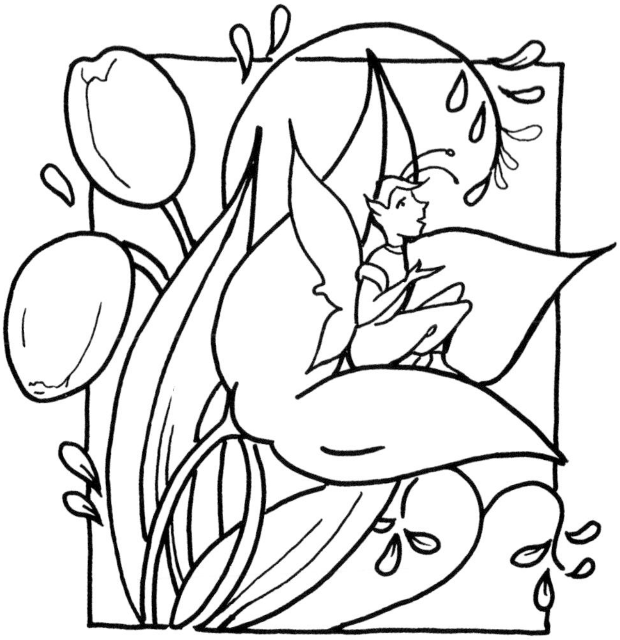
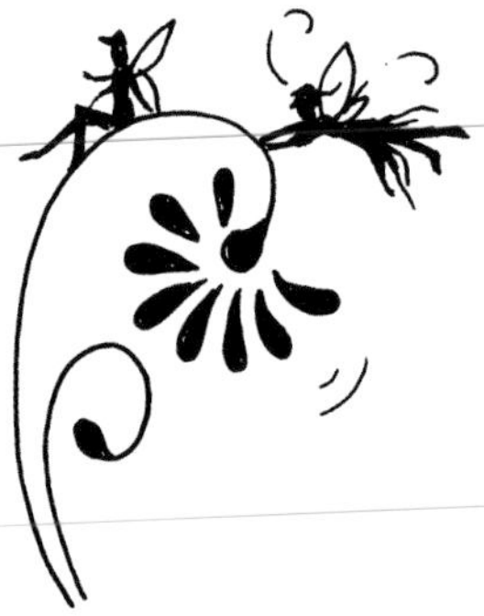
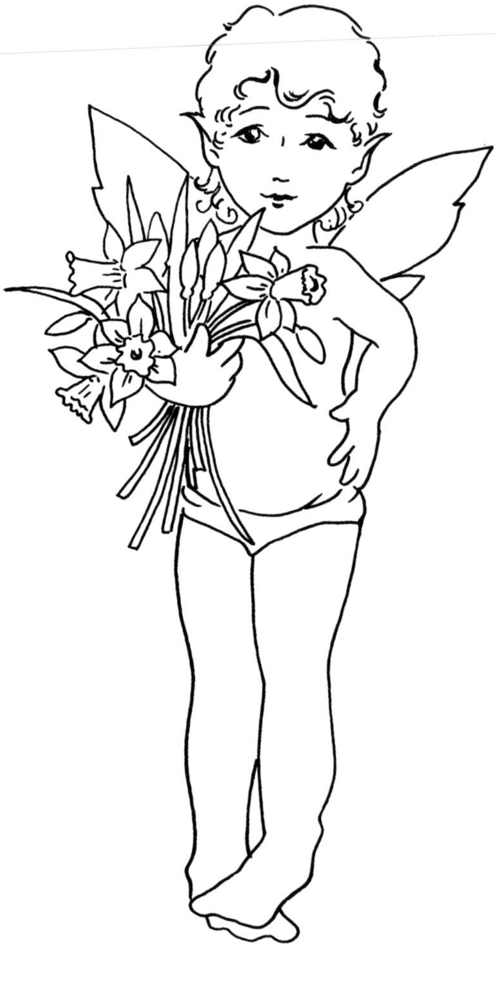
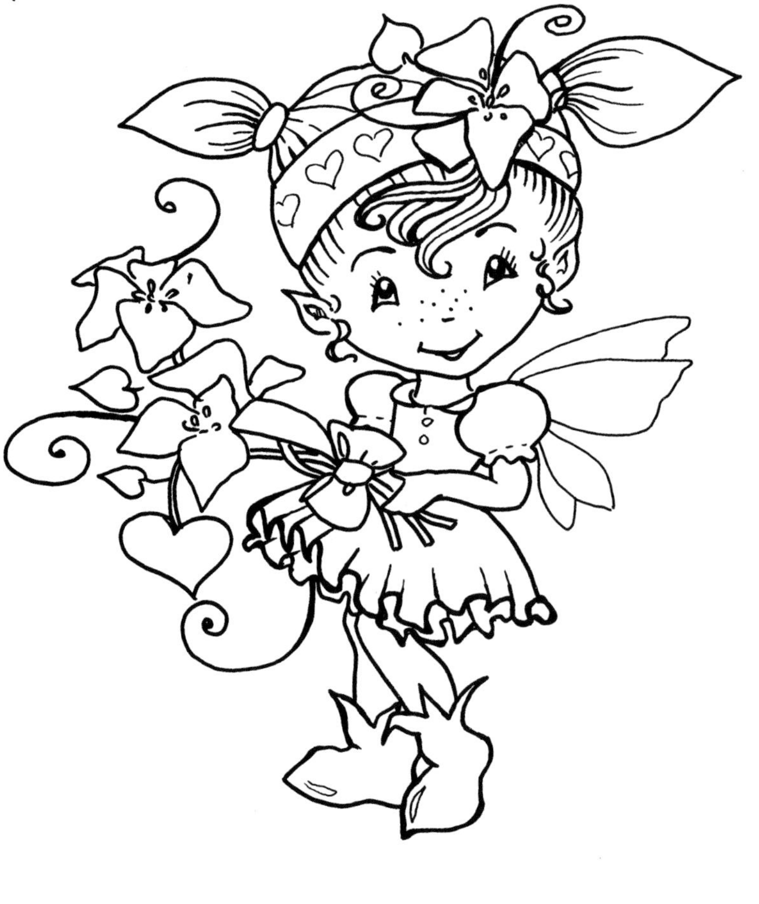

Fairy Tales

There's nothing quite like a story and being read to, and that's how we would have first become familiar with fairies and magical creatures. Stories like *Cinderella*, *Rapunzel* and *The Shoemaker and the Elves* by the Brothers Grimm, *The Little Mermaid* and *Thumbelina* by Hans Christian Andersen, and *Peter Pan* by J M Barrie, have been familiar to most of us since early childhood.

Every country has a wealth of myths and legends to tell, with stories of princes and princesses, witches, wicked stepmothers, spells, magicians, trolls and so on, and many of these figures appear on the following pages. To start with there are trolls and goblins – but not the scary ones – and you'll also find Alice in Wonderland and some of the characters she encountered (page 83), Thumbelina (page 84) and the Little Mermaid (page 85) followed by the characters from *Snow White*, *Sleeping Beauty*, *Cinderella*, *The Snow Queen*, *Rapunzel* and more. See if you can spot characters from other tales too.

Fairy Land

Where do fairies come from? Some believe they live at the bottom of the garden or in a place that is mysteriously neither here nor there. Perhaps they live in their own fairytale land or in woodland dells where they dance between the toadstools in fairy rings, sleep in flowers and take shelter under leaves.

This chapter puts many of its fairies in a setting to suggest a fairy lifestyle. As an example, for transport a fairy might ride a bee-drawn chariot (opposite). She might live in a fairytale castle or a toadstool home (pages 102–103), drink soup from an acorn cup and dance by the light of the moon. And of course, she would have an escort to the dance, so some male fairies are included here too (page 112).

Finishing Touches

Hopefully you've already found a number of fairy motifs for your artwork, and if you read the section at the front of this book you'll get ideas on how to use them. But often you need a few extra bits and pieces to fill an area, attract attention or say something more, and that's exactly what you'll find in this chapter.

Borders, like the ones opposite, are particularly useful for creating a stylish finish. They don't have to be bold – they can be knocked back by using a soft or pale colour and you can add small fairies to them as well. Use the banners and frames on pages 118–119 in the same way. If you want to say it in words, try the fairy alphabet on pages 116–117 or use just one letter – on a greetings card perhaps.

As a little surprise, take a look at the animal fairies on page 120 – remember the Hippo Ballet in Fantasia? These cuties just didn't fit into any category in the book but they just had to go in somewhere, and what better position than the grand finale; enjoy.

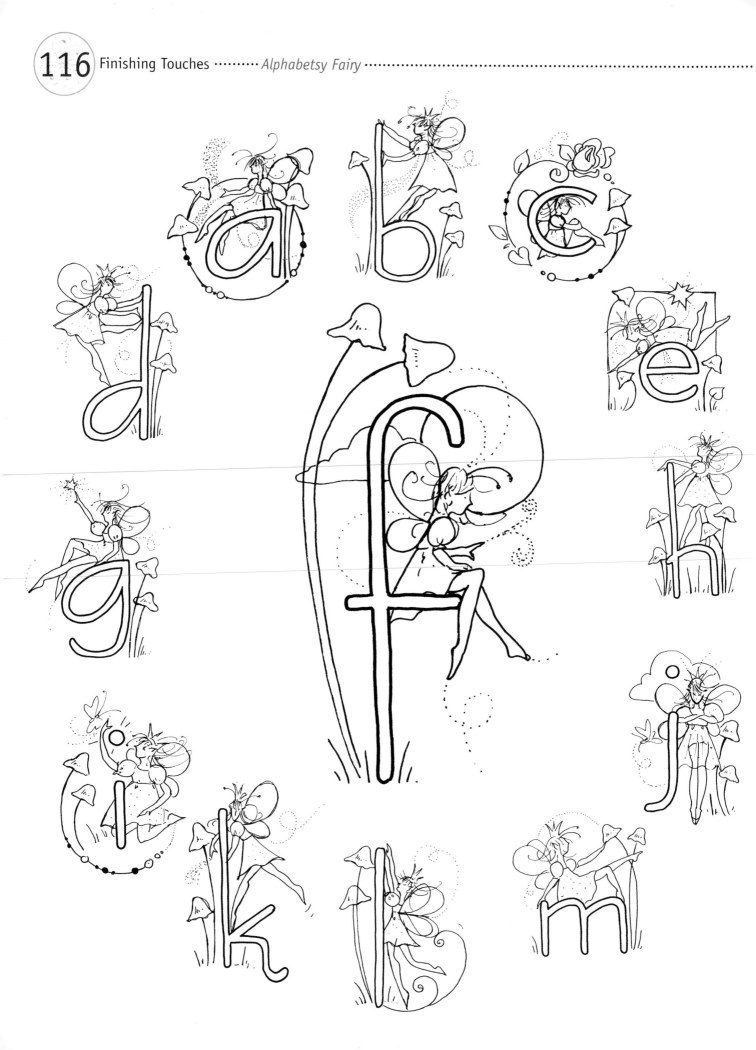

Index

About the author

Sharon Bennett studied graphics and illustration at college before embarking upon a successful career as a packaging designer for various consultancies, eventually becoming Senior Designer for a major confectionary company. In 1986 she started working on a freelance basis in order to divide her time between work and bringing up her family. It was during this time that she moved into the craft world and began to contribute projects to national UK magazines such as *Crafts Beautiful*, and worked on their craft booklets. Sharon has produced four other books for David & Charles, *The Crafter's Design Library: Christmas*, *The Crafter's Design Library: Florals*, *The Crafter's Design Library: Celebrations* and *The Crafter's Design Library: Animals*. Sharon lives with her family in Suffolk, UK.